Drums

Music Makers

THE CHILD'S WORLD®, INC.

Drums

Pamela K. Harris

THE CHILD'S WORLD®, INC.

Library of Congress Cataloging-in-Publication Data
Harris, Pamela K., 1962–
Drums / by Pamela K. Harris.
  p. cm.
Includes index.
Summary: Briefly describes simple drums and how they are made and played.
ISBN 1-56766-683-3 (library reinforced)
1. Drum—Juvenile literature. [1. Drum.] I. Title.
ML1035 .H366 2000
786.9'19—dc21   99-058444

Credits

Translation: Neil Carruthers,
University of Canterbury, Christchurch, New Zealand
Graphic design: Brad Clemmons

Photo Credits

© Corbis Images: 21, 23 (bongos)
© PhotoDisc: 9, 16, 19, 23
© Stone/Tom Main: cover, 3, back cover;
  Jacques Jangoux: 6; Bruno De Hogues: 10;
  Lawrence Migdale: 13; Glen Allison: 15; Joel Simon: 20

Table of Contents

Chapter	Page
The Drum	7
Rhythm Instruments	8
People Making Nature Sounds	11
How Are Drums Made?	12
Drums for Many Reasons	14
Beating a Drum	17
Making Sounds with Movement	18
Different Kinds of Drums	21
More Drums	23
Glossary and Index	24

Crash! Clang! Bang!

Boom! Boom! Boom!

Rat-a-tat-tat!

How are all of these noises made? Drums make these sounds. Drums can make noises as loud as dynamite or as quiet as a whisper. They are musical instruments but they don't play notes. What do drums do?

Rhythm Instruments

Most drums do not play different notes. Instead, they play **rhythm**. Rhythm is the beat of music in a song. Drums help other instruments play notes at the right times during a song. That means the person playing the drums has a very important job!

This *darabuka* drum from Turkey is made from metal. →

People Making Nature Sounds

Thousands of years ago, people learned how to make sounds just like the ones they heard in nature. They sang like birds. They clapped their hands like rain. They stomped their feet like galloping horses. People made drums to sound like the terrifying rumble of thunder.

How Are Drums Made?

People made the first drums from hollow logs. They stretched animal skins across them. Then they made sounds by hitting the skins with their hands or with sticks. Many of today's drums are still made with animal skins stretched across the top. Others use plastic "skins." Instead of logs, today's drums are often made from plastic or metal.

These big *conga* drums are made from wood and animal skins. →

Drums for Many Reasons

People play drums for many different reasons. They play them for dances and to tell stories. They play them when they are happy, scared, or even sad. Some drums are even used to send messages. **Tom-tom** drums came from Africa. Long ago, certain sounds from a tom-tom meant different things. By beating the tom-tom, people could send messages to other people far away.

This *snare drum* is being played by a guard for the Queen of England. ➜

Beating a Drum

Drums belong to a group of musical instruments called **percussion instruments**. You shake, pound, or rub percussion instruments to make sounds. To play a drum, you hit or beat it. You can play a drum by itself or with other instruments. Hitting a drum hard makes a loud sound. Touching it makes a softer noise. Using things such as sticks or your hands changes a drum's sound, too.

← This *taiko* drum from Japan is very big.

Making Sounds with Movement

Drums make sounds by **vibrating**, or moving back and forth. A player hits the top or the skin of the drum, and it vibrates. The bottom part of the drum—the part shaped like a bowl—makes the vibrations louder. The bigger the drum is, the louder the noise can be.

Many drummers put lots of drums together to make a set of drums like this one. This is called a *drum kit*. →

Different Kinds of Drums

There are many different kinds of drums. They can be made from wood or clay. They can be made from metal or bone, too. Some drums are taller than you. Other drums can fit in your hand.

The *taiko* (TY-ee-koh) drum from Japan is so big, it takes two people to carry it! **Bongos** are two drums that are stuck together. Each bongo drum makes a different sound. The *cuica* (koo-EE-kah) drum from Brazil sounds like a monkey. A **tambourine** is a small drum with bells on the side. *Steel drums* come from the Caribbean. They are made from old barrels. Some drums are electric.

← This *steel drum* comes from Trinidad. Can you see which part of the drum might make different notes?

The pounding sound of the *bass drum* is the star of marching bands. The **snare drum** has strings on the bottom. The strings make a buzzing sound when the drum is played. A *kettledrum* looks like big copper bowl. It sounds like thunder! These different shapes and sizes make each drum different and special. Can you make a drum?

More Drums

African cowhide drum

bongos

Native American
frame drum

kettledrum

djembe

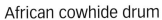

talking drum

23

Glossary

bongos (BONG-ohz)
Bongos are a set of two drums that people play with their hands.

percussion instruments
(per-KUH-shun IN-struh-mentz)
A percussion instrument is an instrument that is played by hitting, shaking, or scraping it.

rhythm (RIH-them)
Rhythm is the beat of the music in a song. Drums make rhythm.

snare drum (SNAYR DRUM)
A snare drum has strings along its underside. The strings make a buzzing or rattling sound when the drum is played.

tambourine (tam-bur-EEN)
A tambourine is a small drum with metal disks on the side. The disks jingle when the tambourine is hit or shaken.

tom-tom (TOM-TOM)
A tom-tom is a small, narrow drum that people play with their hands.

vibrating (VY-bray-ting)
When something is vibrating, it is moving back and forth. Drums make sounds by vibrating.

Index

animal skins, 12

bass drum, 22

bongos, 21

conga, 12

cuica drum, 21

darabuka, 8

drum kit, 18

kettledrum, 22

parts, 18

percussion instruments, 17

playing, 17

rhythm, 8

snare drum, 22

sounds, 7, 11, 17, 18, 21, 22

steel drums, 21

taiko drum, 21

tambourine, 21

tom-tom, 14

vibrating, 18